D0646385

Provinces and Territories of Canada

PRINCE EDWARD ISLAND

— "The Gentle Island" —

Published by Weigl Educational Publishers Limited
6325 10 Street SE
Calgary, Alberta
T2H 2Z9

www.weigl.com

Library and Archives Canada Cataloguing in Publication data available upon request.
Fax 403-233-7769 for the attention of the Publishing Records department.

ISBN 978-1-55388-977-9 (hard cover)
ISBN 978-1-55388-990-8 (soft cover)

Printed in the United States of America
1 2 3 4 5 6 7 8 9 0 13 12 11 10 09

Editor: Heather C. Hudak
Design: Terry Paulhus

All of the Internet URLs given in the book were valid at the time of publication. However, due to the dynamic nature of the Internet, some addresses may have changed, or sites may have ceased to exist since publication. While the author and publisher regret any inconvenience this may cause readers, no responsibility for any such changes can be accepted by either the author or the publisher.

Every reasonable effort has been made to trace ownership and to obtain permission to reprint copyright material. The publishers would be pleased to have any errors or omissions brought to their attention so that they may be corrected in subsequent printings.

Weigl acknowledges Getty Images as its primary image supplier for this title.
National Archives of Canada: pages 27 top, 27 bottom, 28, 29; National Gallery of Canada: page 24; Parks Canada/Barrett & Mackay: page 39 top; Rogers Communications: page 31 bottom; Senator Catherine Callbeck's Office: page 34; Warren Clark: page 25.

We gratefully acknowledge the financial support of the Government of Canada through the Book Publishing Industry Development Program (BPIDP) for our publishing activities.

Contents

Prince Edward Island

Although it takes a little effort to reach the shores of Prince Edward Island, it is well worth the trip. Along with its warm waters, this crescent-shaped island is well known for its warm welcomes. Prince Edward Island is Canada's smallest province, but it is still rich in history, culture, and beauty. The province has emerald fields, deep red soil, white sandy beaches, and a variety of brightly coloured wildflowers. Many visitors are drawn to the island's warm coastal waters and historic villages. In some areas, time seems to have halted, and a number of residents have continued traditional ways of life. In these places, people still play traditional music and make arts and crafts. Prince Edward Island also has modern urban areas, such as Charlottetown and Summerside, where residents enjoy all the **amenities** of a large city.

The West Point Lighthouse is located in Prince County.

Confederation Bridge is considered to be the world's longest bridge over ice-covered waters.
It accommodates two lanes of traffic and has made travel to and from the province much easier for people.

P rince Edward Island is the only province that is entirely detached from the North American mainland. The province is located just off Canada's eastern coast. It lies in the Gulf of Saint Lawrence, which connects to the Atlantic Ocean off the southwestern shore of Newfoundland and the northernmost shore of Nova Scotia. The Northumberland Strait meets Prince Edward Island's southern shoreline. The island's closest neighbours are New Brunswick to the west and Nova Scotia to the southeast. Across the Gulf of Saint Lawrence, to the northwest, is Newfoundland. Prince Edward Island, Nova Scotia, New Brunswick, and Newfoundland are called the Atlantic Provinces.

The Mi'kmaq lived in Prince Edward Island long before Europeans came to the area. They canoed to the island every summer to hunt, fish, and gather nuts and berries. About 500 years

Prince Edward Island's beautiful shorelines and vast green fields draw many visitors to the province.

The capital of Prince Edward Island is Charlottetown.

ago, the first Europeans came to Prince Edward Island, but it took almost 200 years before settlers called the island home. The French were the first to settle and claim the land. Later, the British gained possession of the area. At that time, vast forests covered the island, abundant wildlife roamed the land, and large numbers of fish swam in the waters. Fur trading, farming, forestry, and shipbuilding were among the islanders' early ventures.

When the Canadian federal government was established in 1867, the province could not be convinced to join. Although many people wanted to remain separate from Canada, they finally agreed to join Confederation on July 1, 1873.

Charlottetown is known as Canada's birthplace. It is where the Fathers of Confederation first met to discuss joining the provinces of Canada together to form a country.

The total area of Prince Edward Island is 5,660 square kilometres. It is 224 kilometres long and up to 64 kilometres wide.

When the idea of crossing the Northumberland Strait was in development, a popular plan was to link the island to the mainland by building an underground tunnel.

Cars were not allowed on the island's roads until 1919. Roads were unpaved until the 1930s.

The island was first named "Île Saint-Jean" by the French. In 1799, the British renamed it "Prince Edward Island" after Edward, Duke of Kent.

LAND AND CLIMATE

Thousands of years ago, glaciers covered Prince Edward Island. As the glaciers melted, they deposited debris, comprised mainly of red sandstone. This debris covered most of the island. These sandstone deposits give the island's fertile soil its rich, red colour.

The island is part of a lowland section of the Appalachian Region, called the Gulf of Saint Lawrence Plain. The Gulf of Saint Lawrence Plain is a low depression. Along the southern and western coasts, cliffs of red sandstone meet the choppy waters of the Northumberland Strait. The northern side of the island, which faces the Gulf of Saint Lawrence, has sandy white beaches along with extensive sand dunes.

Until recently, one of the province's most popular sites was Elephant Rock, a bright red landmark that was created by the winds and pounding waves of the ocean. The elephant's trunk fell into the sea in 1998.

Gently rolling plains cover much of the island's interior, with very few hills that rise over 60 metres. The highest point in the province is located at Springton, in Queens County. There, the land reaches about 152 metres.

Prince Edward Island's maritime location and warm ocean currents moderate its climate. It is generally very humid on the island, with long, mild winters and cool, breezy summers. The average January temperature in Prince Edward Island is −7° Celsius. The island's average July temperature is 19° Celsius. Unlike other Atlantic provinces, Prince Edward Island has very little fog.

Two of the bays that cut into Prince Edward Island include Malpeque and Hillsborough.

There are almost no freshwater lakes in Prince Edward Island. However, there are many long bays and inlets along the southern and eastern coasts.

NATURAL RESOURCES

More than half of the island is used for agriculture.

Soil is the island's main natural resource. Prince Edward Island's red soil is excellent for growing crops—especially potato crops. Potato farming is a thriving business in Prince Edward Island. The area's rich soil, clean air and water, and long winters provide a suitable environment for potato crops.

No large mineral deposits have been discovered in Prince Edward Island, but there are small amounts of coal, uranium, and other minerals in the area. Some natural gas has been found in the northeast, but there is not enough to make exploration worthwhile. The province's most valuable mineral products are sand and gravel, obtained by open-pit mining.

KEEP CONNECTED

Potato farming is a thriving industry in Prince Edward Island. Learn more at **www.peipotato.org**.

With about 99 percent of the province's forest areas being privately owned, there is almost no commercial forestry in Prince Edward Island.

Prince Edward Island pays one of the highest prices for electricity in Canada because it does not have sources of hydroelectric power, coal, or oil.

Since the island lacks large rivers, **hydropower** has not been developed. Instead, fossil fuels are burned to generate electricity. Islanders are also supplied with electricity from a submarine cable that connects to New Brunswick.

GET THE FACTS

In the mid-1800s, shipbuilding was a thriving industry in Prince Edward Island. At that time, the island's large forests provided much of the lumber.

By 1758, 4,850 hectares of original forest had been cut down in Prince Edward Island.

The development of fox farming in the late 1880s brought money to the island. Charles Dalton and Robert Oulton were the first in the area to raise foxes for their pelts. Today, the province's most valuable fur is mink.

PLANTS AND ANIMALS

The provincial tree is the red oak. It grew in abundance when Jacques Cartier came to the island in 1534, but its numbers have greatly declined since then.

The provincial flower is the lady's slipper, which is a type of orchid. The petals of the pink lady's slipper are pouch-shaped, like a slipper.

The plant life in Prince Edward Island, although thriving, is not as diverse as it is in other Canadian provinces. This is because the climate and terrain differ very little across the island. However, the fertile red soil does manage to sustain many different kinds of grasses, wildflowers, and trees. Wildflowers such as brown-eyed Susans, buttercups, mayflowers, primroses, violets, wild asters, goldenrods, and daisies flourish all over the island. Irish moss can be seen growing in some of the coastal areas.

It is hard to believe that dense forests once covered Prince Edward Island. Little remains of the island's original forests because most of its trees were cut down in the eighteenth and nineteenth centuries for shipbuilding, or to clear land for agriculture. Even over the last 100 years, the upland forests have dwindled. Efforts to restore parts of the forests are being made. Today, the island is dotted with small woodlands, consisting mainly of spruce and birch trees. Other trees in the province include evergreen, maple, birch, oak, beech, ash, and elm. In some areas, orchards of apple and cherry trees grow.

Red foxes are abundant throughout the province. Many live in the inland forests of Prince Edward Island National Park.

Prince Edward Island's skies, sea, cliffs, and beaches are often crowded with birds. There are over 330 bird species on the island. Among them are the great blue heron, wood duck, barred owl, Cape May warbler, sharp-tailed sparrow, and the piping plover. Sea-going birds can be seen in many parts of the island, but especially near East Point and North Cape. There, the double-breasted cormorant bobs offshore.

There are many marine mammals off the island's shores. Atlantic white-sided dolphins and harbour porpoises frolic in the Northumberland Strait, just off High Bank and White Sands. Seals are another common sight. Harbour seals and grey seals are often seen near Panmure Island in the winter.

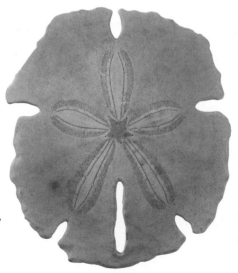

Sand dollars, as well as moon snails, sponges, and moon jellies, live just off the island's rocky shores.

The waters surrounding Prince Edward Island are home to many marine mammals, including seals.

The provincial bird is the blue jay. It was chosen by a province-wide public vote in 1976.

The most common mammals in Prince Edward Island are the raccoon, red squirrel, chipmunk, snowshoe hare, muskrat, red fox, and beaver. There are no large mammals on the island. The black bear, which disappeared from the island in the 1920s, was the last large mammal.

GET THE FACTS

Fish and **crustaceans** found in the sea around the island include scallops, oysters, clams, cods, lobsters, and herrings.

Although they have disappeared from the island, walruses were a common sight in the early 1700s.

The piping plover is the only endangered species nesting in Prince Edward Island.

Although it was once covered with tall hardwood forests, Prince Edward Island is now home to only a small number of wood lots. Most of these wooded areas are surrounded by farmland.

At Prince Edward Island National Park, there are inland spruce and birch forests as well as saltwater marshes and inland ponds. The park provides a home for muskrats, raccoons, skunks, and minks.

TOURISM

Many tourists come to Prince Edward Island to enjoy its sparkling white beaches, quaint villages, energetic festivals, and rich heritage. In the summer, more than 700,000 people flock to the island, and that number is increasing every year. Deep-sea fishing, sailing, and swimming are enjoyed in the warm, coastal waters.

The Charlottetown Festival, held at the Confederation Centre of the Arts, runs from June to September. It features a variety of music and plays, but the highlight is the musical play, *Anne of Green Gables*. The musical has been performed every summer since 1965 at the Confederation Centre of the Arts. It is Canada's longest-running musical production. Many tourists associate Prince Edward Island with Lucy Maud Montgomery's popular fictional character, Anne Shirley. Tales of Anne's mishaps and adventures introduced Prince Edward Island to readers around the world, and these stories are now responsible for bringing many people to the island.

Anne has inspired another popular festival in Prince Edward Island. Cavendish hosts the Lucy Maud Montgomery Festival, which is a literary festival held from July to August. It honours Anne's creator and includes a barn dance, a corn boil, traditional music, and a memorial service for Lucy Maud Montgomery.

Fans of the novel *Anne of Green Gables* may visit Lucy Maud Montgomery's home in Cavendish.

Many businesses, including restaurants and hotels, serve the large numbers of tourists who visit the island in the summer.

From late May to October, many golfers gather their clubs and head to Prince Edward Island. The province is known as a world-class golfing destination and has many beautiful, well-groomed golf courses.

During lobster season, many visitors come to the island to sample fresh lobster meat.

KEEP CONNECTED

Fishing is one of Prince Edward Island's principal industries, with lobsters being the province's most important catch. Learn more about Prince Edward Island's lobster fishing season at **www.tourismpei.com/pei-lobster-season**.

Agriculture plays a significant role in Prince Edward Island's economy. Farmland makes up over half of the province's land area. Potatoes are the province's largest crop. Some potatoes are produced for table use, or domestic **consumption**. Quebec and Ontario buy the most table-use potatoes. The province also produces seed potatoes that are exported to over fifteen different countries. Seed potatoes are planted in the ground and used to grow potato plants. Other important crops on the island include barley, tobacco, and vegetables. The province also produces beef, pork, and dairy products.

Irish moss is gathered and sold as a thickening ingredient for some cosmetics and food products. It is also processed and found in ice cream, pie fillings, and toothpaste.

The fishing industry employs many people in the province. Prince Edward Island is well known for its high-quality seafood, especially lobster. People all over the country look forward to lobster season, when they can taste the fresh, sweet lobster that is caught off the island's shores. Other valuable catches include mackerel, tuna, cod, sole, flounder, scallops, and oysters.

The manufacturing industry is important to the province. Prince Edward Island processes most of its own agricultural and fish products. It also makes printed materials, wood and metal products, fertilizers, and medical instruments.

Prince Edward Island has more than 2,000 farms.

GOODS AND SERVICES

The University of Prince Edward Island was created when Prince of Wales College and Saint Dunstan's University merged in 1969. About 2,900 full-time and part-time students study at the University of Prince Edward Island. These students may earn degrees in many areas, including business and veterinary medicine.

Island residents are served by one main library system, with more than 20 library branches scattered throughout the province.

Prince Edward Island provides many local services to residents and visitors. The service sector includes health care, education, communication industries, hotels, and restaurants. The largest hospital in the province is the Queen Elizabeth Hospital in Charlottetown. Eight smaller hospitals are also found on the island. Islanders are served by a health-care plan that offers many medical and hospital services at little or no cost.

There is only one university in the province, the University of Prince Edward Island. It was founded in 1969, and offers students programs in arts, sciences, business, and education. The island also has one community college, the Holland College of Applied Arts. There are about 65 elementary and secondary schools in the province.

KEEP CONNECTED
Visitors do not have to pay a fare when they take the Northumberland Ferry or the Confederation Bridge to Prince Edward Island. However, they do have to pay a fare to get off the island. To learn more about travelling to Prince Edward Island, check out **www.tourismpei.com/getting-to-pei.**

The province caters to many tourists who visit each year. Tourism is an important industry on the island, and many residents earn an income by renting cottages or offering bed and breakfasts. Many others find employment at hotels and restaurants. There are fewer job opportunities in the winter, during off-season, when only a small number of tourists visit the area.

To learn about community events, Prince Edward Island residents may choose between two local daily newspapers. Both the *Journal-Pioneer* and *The Guardian* keep island-dwellers well informed. The two newspapers have existed for many years, with the *Journal-Pioneer* from Summerside dating back to 1865, and *The Guardian* from Charlottetown dating back to 1887.

Potatoes and seed potatoes are Prince Edward Island's main export.

GET THE FACTS

There are nine radio stations and four television stations in the province.

In 1994, the Anne of Green Gables Licensing Authority was established to protect the image rights of the fictional Anne. The Authority reviews all applications of Anne-related products. Those which are licensed bear a distinctive Anne Authority logo.

There are more than 250 festivals and events in Prince Edward Island throughout the year.

The province has a sales tax of 10 percent, which is added after the nation's 5 percent goods and services tax.

FIRST NATIONS

The Mi'kmaq traded goods with European settlers. Animal pelts were traded in return for items such as clothes, kettles, and guns.

Most of the information about Prince Edward Island's first inhabitants has been learned from archaeological findings, Aboriginal legends, and the writings of missionaries and explorers. It is believed that Paleo-Indians lived on the island about 10,000 years ago.

The Mi'kmaq are descended from the island's first dwellers. They named Prince Edward Island *Abegweit*, which means "cradled on the waves." In the past, the Mi'kmaq were hunter-gatherers. During the winter, they hunted along the rivers, where they found bear, deer, moose, caribou, and beaver. In the summer, they moved toward the ocean coast. Here, they fished, caught seabirds, and speared porpoises. They also gathered berries and other plants to use as food and medicine.

Early Mi'kmaq lived in **wigwams** and spoke a form of the Algonquian language. When Acadian settlers and French fur traders came to the island, the Mi'kmaq taught them where to look for food and how to make medicines from local plants. The French traders and the Mi'kmaq were allies for some time. With the arrival of the British, the Mi'kmaq lost their hunting grounds, along with many of their rights.

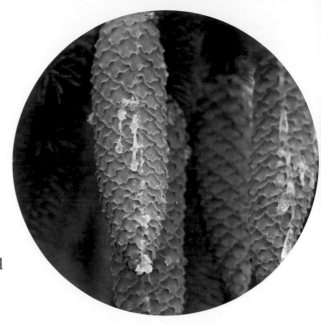

Early canoes made by the Mi'kmaq measured about 8 metres long and were made out of birch and cedar. To protect their canoes from leaks, the Mi'kmaq used spruce gum, which was chewed, boiled in fat, and then applied to the wood.

The Mi'kmaq lived in wigwams in the summer, and warmer birch bark-covered wigwams in the winter.

EXPLORERS

The first European to set foot on Prince Edward Island was Jacques Cartier, a French explorer. On June 30, 1534, he and his crew landed on the island's northern shore. He explored the area for two days, thinking he had landed on the mainland. When he sighted the Mi'kmaq paddling

In the early 1600s, Samuel de Champlain explored and claimed much of eastern Canada for France. Throughout his travels, he gained the help and friendship of many Aboriginal Peoples.

down a river in canoes, he named the river Canoe River. Cartier claimed the island for France and then sailed home.

Samuel de Champlain, a French explorer, named Prince Edward Island, "Île Saint-Jean." Although Champlain claimed the island for France again in 1603, there were no permanent settlers until about 1720. Many Europeans fished in the area, but none stayed. From 1653 to 1720, France granted the island to four different men, hoping they would bring settlers to the area. When an owner failed to attract colonists to the area, the property was granted to another candidate. Finally, about 250 colonists sailed to the island from France, settling along the coast.

When Europeans first came to the east coast, there were about 18,000 Mi'kmaq living in the area.

GET THE FACTS

In 1650, France granted fishing rights in the Gulf of Saint Lawrence and along the Atlantic coast to a French trading company called La Compagnie de la Nouvelle France.

Throughout the 17th century, the island was used as a base for seasonal fishers, but no one settled in the area.

EARLY SETTLERS

In order to develop the island, many early settlers were forced to clear the area of its vast, thriving forests.

Landowner Thomas Douglas, Earl of Selkirk, was responsible for one of the first major Scottish settlements on Prince Edward Island.

Ile Saint-Jean became a British colony in 1763. When the British took control, they drove out most of the French inhabitants. The British changed the island's name to Saint John's Island, and governed it as part of the Nova Scotia colony. Two years after the British took control of the island, it was divided into 67 lots which were then granted in a lottery to British nobles. These owners were called **proprietors**. On July 23, 1767, the British government selected 100 men to participate in the lottery. All of the participants wrote their names on slips of paper, which were drawn, one by one, until all the parcels of land were given away. The British king expected the proprietors to encourage settlement and to develop the island. In 1769, the island became a separate British colony—it was awarded its own government, independent of Nova Scotia's.

Early farming practices were time-consuming and difficult. Farmers planted seeds by hand, harvested crops with crescent-shaped knives called scythes, and gathered crops with rakes.

For many years, few proprietors brought settlers to the island. In fact, many prevented settlers from coming by refusing to sell them land. Since settlers could obtain free land in other parts of North America, the island remained sparsely populated and underdeveloped.

In 1803, Thomas Douglas, the Earl of Selkirk, brought 800 Scottish settlers to the island. After this large wave of settlers, more and more people followed. Conditions were harsh at first, and many early settlers came unprepared for the island's wilderness. In order to begin farming the land, it had to be cleared of trees and stumps. The work was difficult and slow, but settlers were eventually able to provide for themselves. By 1820, there were about 15,000 people living on the island.

Most of the early pioneers were English, Scottish, Irish, and Acadian. Many lived in small log cabins. Large fireplaces kept them warm in the winter. The settlers prevented drafts by stuffing the cracks in their log homes with moss and wood chips.

The American Revolution, which took place between 1775 and 1783, was critical to the history of Prince Edward Island. After the war, a few hundred Scottish settlers migrated to the island along with hundreds of British settlers who had been involved in the fighting.

Many people lived in small communities, and neighbours helped one another through difficult times. Still, island life was full of many chores and tasks. Pioneers grew, hunted, and caught their own food. They also made their own clothing, soaps, medicines, and candles.

GET THE FACTS

Several early settlers in Prince Edward Island built dikes to help protect their farmland.

In 1851, the British government granted Prince Edward Island residents control of their own local affairs.

After Prince Edward Island entered Confederation, the Canadian government passed the Land Purchase Act. This act gave the province enough money to buy out the proprietors' lands. People then bought the land from the province.

POPULATION

Charlottetown has the province's highest population, with more than 32,000 residents.

Unlike most other Canadian provinces and territories, Prince Edward Island's population has grown very little over the last 100 years. The island's slow economy has forced many residents to move away in search of employment. With so many young people leaving the province in search of work, the number of people over the age of 65 has been steadily increasing.

Prince Edward Island is the most densely populated province in the country because it is so small. With an average density of 24 people per square kilometre, it is difficult to avoid one's neighbours. Most residents are of British ancestry, and about one-quarter of the people have some French origin. Almost all island-dwellers were born in Canada.

Summerside has more than 14,500 people.

About 45 percent of Prince Edward Island's residents live in urban areas, especially in Charlottetown and Summerside. The rest of the population lives in rural districts.

About 400 Mi'kmaq live on reservations in Prince Edward Island. There are four Mi'kmaq reservations in Prince Edward Island.

Prince Edward Island's early settlers cleared much of its vast forests so that they could farm. Today, descendants of these settlers continue to farm the land.

Peake's Quay, in Charlottetown, is a popular gathering place for many islanders.

POLITICS AND GOVERNMENT

In January 1993, Catherine Callbeck, Prince Edward Island's Liberal Party leader, became the first woman in Canadian history to become a premier. She held that position until October 1996.

Prince Edward Island rejected Confederation in 1867, when many other Canadian provinces joined. At that time, islanders were afraid of losing their unique culture and identity. They thought it would be sacrificed by joining Canada. Still, on July 1, 1873, Prince Edward Island joined the Canadian union, becoming the seventh province.

On the federal level, four members of Parliament represent the province in the House of Commons. When Prince Edward Island joined Confederation, it was entitled to six members of Parliament. However, its limited population growth over the years has cost the province two members.

The Legislative Assembly makes the provincial laws. It consists of 27 members, who serve up to five-year terms. Members are elected from 16 electoral districts.

In 1864, Province House hosted a historic meeting that led to the 1867 formation of Canada. Today, the province's Legislative Assembly continues to meet in this Charlottetown building.

The province's premier presides over the executive council, also known as the Cabinet. The Cabinet usually has 10 members at one time. Each member heads a different government department.

There are three levels of local government in Prince Edward Island—community, town, and city. Charlottetown, along with seven other large communities, is governed under elected mayors and councillors. Either elected chairpersons or councillors govern about 75 smaller municipalities.

The province has one Provincial Court and a small claims court, but no county courts. The Supreme Court is the highest court in the province.

Prince Edward Island's provincial motto is *Parva Sub Ingenti*, which means "the small under the protection of the great."

The Charlottetown Accord was signed in 1992, in the city of Charlottetown. This accord was designed to amend the Canadian Constitution. It was defeated in a national vote the same year.

The island is divided into three counties—Kings, Queens, and Prince.

In January 1988, a **plebiscite** was held to decide whether or not people wanted a fixed link between Prince Edward Island and New Brunswick—33,229 voted for a fixed link, while 22,472 voted against the idea.

CULTURAL GROUPS

Prince Edward Island has a variety of cultural groups that celebrate their heritage with pride. About 12 percent of the province's residents are of Acadian ancestry. Acadians are the descendants of the first French colonists of North America. They are known for their French language, Roman Catholic religion, traditional clothing, and festivals such as Chandeleur and Mardi Gras.

The earliest Acadians lived in the present-day provinces of Nova Scotia, New Brunswick, Prince Edward Island, and small parts of Quebec. The first Acadians to Prince Edward Island came in 1720, settling in Port La Joie, near Charlottetown. During the following century, the British forced many Acadians off the island's soil. In fact, many were deported back to France in the mid-1700s. Those who were able to stay on the island were scattered throughout the region and became isolated. Many lost their traditional language. Today, only about 5 percent of the population of Prince Edward Island has French as their first language. Still, there has been a strong promotion of Acadian culture in recent years. In 1965, a monument honouring the first Acadian pioneers was erected on the Port La Joie/Fort Amherst National Historic Site.

To help preserve their identity, the Acadians continue to wear their traditional clothing for special events.

Most islanders are of Scottish, Irish, or English ancestry. In the mid-19th century, Scottish people made up half of the total population. Most immigrated to Prince Edward Island from the Western Highlands and the **Hebrides**. They spoke Gaelic and wore tartan kilts, which showed their loyalty to their family-based **clan**. Today, residents of Scottish descent make up the largest ethnic group within the province. Many still practise their lively traditions. A major Scottish festival is held in Summerside every June. Called the Summerside Highland Gathering, it features pipe bands, Scottish drumming, Highland dancers, fiddling, stepdancing, and traditional Highland athletic events.

Highland dancing competitions are a part of many Highland gatherings.

GET THE FACTS

Acadians celebrate their culture throughout the province with festivals and lively parades.

Pipe band competitions are a popular feature of the annual Summerside Highland Gathering.

About two-thirds of the Acadians who were deported back to France in the mid-1700s did not survive the voyage.

People from Lebanon came to Prince Edward Island in the late 1880s. Early Lebanese settlers made a living by travelling to farms selling goods such as tea and clothing.

There are many different religious faiths practised in Prince Edward Island. The largest group is Catholic followed by Presbyterian, Anglican, Baptist, and Jewish.

Prince Edward Island's first French-language newspaper, called *L'Impartial*, was published in 1893.

More than 60 different nationalities live in Prince Edward Island. This is less than any other Canadian province.

ARTS AND ENTERTAINMENT

Prince Edward Island's strong British and French heritage is clearly expressed through its music. The province is home to many musical styles, including **Celtic**, Acadian, country, **bluegrass**, blues, pop, and classical. Musical performers play in venues that range from local clubs to concert halls. The province has produced many talented and popular artists, including Stompin' Tom Connors, Lennie Gallant, Gene MacLellan, and Nancy White. In the province's earlier days, songwriter Lawrence Doyle gained recognition for his songs about island life and history.

There is also an active theatre scene on the island. Charlottetown is home to the largest theatre on the island, housed in the Confederation Centre of the Arts. Smaller theatre companies include the King's Playhouse in Georgetown and the Victoria Playhouse and Harbourfront Jubilee Theatre in Summerside. These playhouses offer an array of productions, including children's theatre and original plays.

The Confederation Centre Art Gallery displays works of art that explore Canada's diverse cultural heritage. It is the largest public art gallery in Atlantic Canada.

Although writer Lucy Maud Montgomery's book, *Anne of Green Gables*, has made Prince Edward Island famous, the island has been blessed with many talented authors. Writer Sir Andrew Macphail and poets Milton Acorn and Elaine Harrison have all written about life on Prince Edward Island. Elaine Harrison's highly regarded poem, "I am an Island that Dreams," communicates her love for the province.

Robert Harris is the province's best-known visual artist. He was an expert portrait painter who studied art in London, Boston, and Paris. His famous painting, called *Fathers of Confederation*, was completed in 1884. It was hung in Ottawa's Parliament Building and duplicated on Canadian postage stamps. Today, there are many visual arts and crafts within the province. The Confederation Centre Art Gallery in Charlottetown features works by local artists, as well as a large collection of Robert Harris's art.

A large Mi'kmaq powwow is held at Panmure Island every August. People can watch drumming demonstrations and dancing, and sample traditional foods.

GET THE FACTS

The Confederation Centre of the Arts houses theatres, an art gallery, and a public library. It was built in 1964 as a memorial to the Fathers of Confederation.

At the Indian River Festival at Indian River, classical concerts and choral performers thrill audiences.

The Rollo Bay Fiddle Festival features fiddlers and traditional musicians from across North America.

Lucy Maud Montgomery wrote the *Island Hymn* in 1908. In the song, Prince Edward Island is called "Fair Island of the Sea."

Bluegrass lovers may attend the PEI Bluegrass and Old Time Music Festival in July.

Robert Harris's painting, *The Fathers of Confederation*, was destroyed when Ottawa's Parliament Building burned down in 1916. He had kept early sketches of the painting so it could be reproduced. By that time, Harris was unable to paint due to poor eyesight.

Outdoor activities in Prince Edward Island include golfing, sea-kayaking, clam-digging, bird-watching, deep-sea fishing, and camping.

Many people enjoy camping along the shoreline. There, they can watch for seals and porpoises.

Prince Edward Island's gentle terrain, open spaces, and mild climate make it an ideal setting for outdoor pursuits. People flock to the island to enjoy its numerous cycling trails. The province has earned a reputation as one of the best places to cycle in Canada. With its beautiful scenery and well-kept trails, it is easy to see why. The most popular place to ride a bike on the island is Confederation Trail. This trail takes cyclists on a whirlwind of adventures. They journey through wetlands, hardwood forests, hayfields, and little villages. For more courageous cyclists, it is easy to plan a trip on the island that takes weeks to complete.

Along with cycling, many people hike and jog along the island's twisting trails. In the winter, Confederation Trail opens for snowmobilers and cross-country skiers. There are also two equestrian trails on the island that cater to those who prefer to discover Prince Edward Island on horseback.

Brad Richards began playing with Tampa Bay in the 2000 to 2001 NHL season. He was acquired to play for Dallas on February 26, 2008.

There are no professional sports teams in Prince Edward Island. Still, the island has provided Canada's National Hockey League (NHL) with many strong players. Among Prince Edward Island's NHL hockey stars are Gerard Gallant, Bobby and Billy MacMillan, and John Chabot. Also, the University of Prince Edward Island has popular soccer, basketball, and hockey teams that have ranked among the best in Canada over the years.

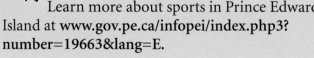

KEEP CONNECTED

Learn more about sports in Prince Edward Island at www.gov.pe.ca/infopei/index.php3?number=19663&lang=E.

Harness racing is such a popular sporting event in Prince Edward Island that the province has earned the title "The Kentucky of Canada."

Harness racing has been a popular sporting event in Prince Edward Island for many years. The largest attraction in harness racing is the Gold Cup and Saucer Race, which is held every August in Charlottetown during the Old Home Week Provincial Exhibition. Winners of this race return home with as much as $60,000.

GET THE FACTS

One of the world's top female golfers, Lorie Kane, grew up in Prince Edward Island.

Confederation Trail was built on an old railway bed and spans the entire province.

The Gold Cup and Saucer Race is one of eastern Canada's most highly regarded harness races. It is held every year at the Charlottetown Driving Park.

Many beaches line the island's north shore, including Brackley Beach and Blooming Point.

Greenwich, in Prince Edward Island National Park, is the site of fascinating sand dunes and wetlands. It is also home to many shorebirds.

CANADA

Canada is a vast nation, and each province and territory has its own unique features. This map shows important information about each of Canada's 10 provinces and three territories, including when they joined Confederation, their size, population, and capital city. For more information about Canada, visit **http://canada.gc.ca**.

Alberta
Entered Confederation: 1905
Capital: Edmonton
Area: 661,848 sq km
Population: 3,632,483

British Columbia
Entered Confederation: 1871
Capital: Victoria
Area: 944,735 sq km
Population: 4,419,974

Manitoba
Entered Confederation: 1870
Capital: Winnipeg
Area: 647,797 sq km
Population: 1,213,815

New Brunswick
Entered Confederation: 1867
Capital: Fredericton
Area: 72,908 sq km
Population: 748,319

Newfoundland and Labrador
Entered Confederation: 1949
Capital: St. John's
Area: 405,212 sq km
Population: 508,990

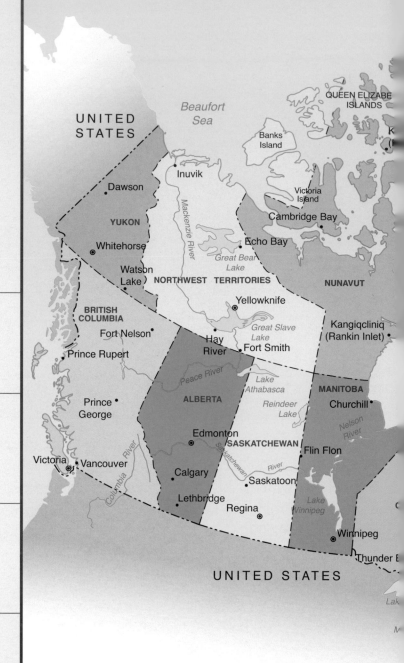

SYMBOLS OF PRINCE EDWARD ISLAND

FLAG
COAT OF ARMS
FLOWER
Pink Lady's slipper

Map labels

Alert

0 200 400 Kilometers
0 200 400 Miles

Baffin Bay

Baffin Island

Davis Strait

Iqaluit (Frobisher Bay)

Ivujivik

Labrador Sea

dson ay

NEWFOUNDLAND

Schefferville

Happy Valley-Goose Bay

Island of Newfoundland

Chisasibi (Fort George)

Gander

Saint John's

QUEBEC

Sept-Iles

Gulf of St. Lawrence

St. Pierre and Miquelon (FRANCE)

Moosonee

PRINCE EDWARD ISLAND

Sydney

Chibougamau

NEW BRUNSWICK

Charlottetown

Fredericton

Quebec

Sudbury

Sherbrooke

Montreal

Saint John

Halifax

NOVA SCOTIA

Ottawa

Lake Huron

Lake Ontario

Toronto
Hamilton
London

Lake Erie

BIRD
Blue Jay

TREE
Red Oak

SOIL
Charlottetown Soil

Northwest Territories
Entered Confederation: 1870
Capital: Yellowknife
Area: 1,346,106 sq km
Population: 42,940

Nova Scotia
Entered Confederation: 1867
Capital: Halifax
Area: 55,284 sq km
Population: 939,531

Nunavut
Entered Confederation: 1999
Capital: Iqaluit
Area: 2,093,190 sq km
Population: 531,556

Ontario
Entered Confederation: 1867
Capital: Toronto
Area: 1,076,395 sq km
Population: 12,986,857

Prince Edward Island
Entered Confederation: 1873
Capital: Charlottetown
Area: 5,660 sq km
Population: 140,402

Quebec
Entered Confederation: 1867
Capital: Quebec City
Area: 1,542,056 sq km
Population: 7,782,561

Saskatchewan
Entered Confederation: 1905
Capital: Regina
Area: 651,036 sq km
Population: 1,023,810

Yukon
Entered Confederation: 1898
Capital: Whitehorse
Area: 482,443 sq km
Population: 33,442

BRAIN TEASERS

Test your knowledge of Prince Edward Island by trying to answer these boggling brain teasers!

1 Multiple Choice

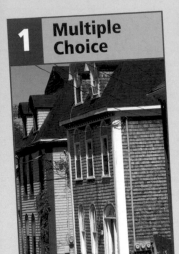

What is the capital of PEI?
a) Summerside
b) Montague
c) Alberton
d) Charlottetown

2 True or False?

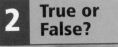

PEI is the only province that is completely detached from the North American mainland.

3 Multiple Choice

What is the provincial flower?
a) rose
b) pink lady's slipper
c) carnation
d) tulip

4 Multiple Choice

What is PEI's main natural resource?
a) minerals
b) soil
c) lumber
d) water

5 Multiple Choice

What is PEI's most grown crop?
a) wheat
b) cucumbers
c) potatoes
d) canola

6 True or False?

There is a great deal of commercial forestry in PEI.

7 Multiple Choice

Which popular book series made PEI famous?
a) *Lord of the Rings*
b) *Anne of Green Gables*
c) *The Witch, The Lion, and the Wardrobe*
d) *Little House on the Prairie*

8 Multiple Choice

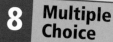

Which of the following is NOT a major industry in PEI?
a) farming
b) fishing
c) oil
d) manufacturing

1. D, Charlottetown is the capital of PEI.   2. True   3. B, The pink lady's slipper is the provincial flower of PEI.   4. B, Soil is the island's main natural resource. 5. C, Potatoes are PEI's most grown crop.   6. False, With 99 percent of the province's forest area privately owned, there is practically no commercial forestry in PEI.   7. B, The book series *Anne of Green Gables* made PEI famous.   8. C, Oil is not a major industry in PEI.

MORE INFORMATION

GLOSSARY

allies: groups that are united, usually against a common cause

amenities: modern features

bluegrass: a form of country music

Celtic: relating to people of Scottish descent; also linked to people of Irish and Welsh descent

clan: a Scottish group with common ancestors

consumption: to use for food

crustaceans: hard-shelled aquatic animals, such as crab, shrimp, and lobster

Hebrides: a group of islands off Scotland

hydropower: electricity gained by gathering water power

plebiscite: a direct vote on important public matters

proprietors: people who own or hold property

wigwams: tents made of animal skins or bark draped over long poles

BOOKS

Banting, Erinn. *Canadian Geographic Regions: The Appalachian.* Calgary: Weigl Educational Publishers Limited, 2006.

Beehag, Graham. *Canadian Industries: Fishing.* Calgary: Weigl Educational Publishers Limited, 2007.

Craats, Rennay. *Canadian Sites and Symbols: Prince Edward Island.* Calgary: Weigl Educational Publishers Limited, 2004.

Nault, Jennifer. *Canada's Land and People: Prince Edward Island.* Calgary: Weigl Educational Publishers Limited, 2008.

WEBSITES

The Government of Prince Edward Island
www.gov.pe.ca

A Guide to Prince Edward Island
www.peionline.com

Atlantic Canada Visitor Information
www.atlanticcanada.worldweb.com

Some websites stay current longer than others. To find information on Prince Edward Island, use your Internet search engine to look up such topics as "Charlottetown," "Summerside," "Confederation Bridge," or any other topic you want to research.

INDEX